The Wish Fisher

by Holly Harper  illustrated by Alicia Borges

OXFORD
UNIVERSITY PRESS
AUSTRALIA & NEW ZEALAND

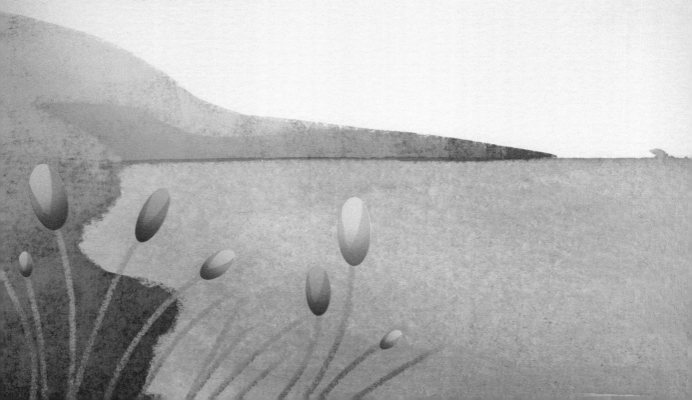

OXFORD
UNIVERSITY PRESS

Oxford University Press is a department of the University of Oxford.
It furthers the University's objective of excellence in research, scholarship,
and education by publishing worldwide. Oxford is a registered trademark
of Oxford University Press in the UK and in certain other countries.

Published in Australia by
Oxford University Press
Level 8, 737 Bourke Street, Docklands, Victoria 3008, Australia

ISBN 9780190317591

Series Advisor: Nikki Gamble
Designed by Ana Cosma
Illustrated by Alicia Borges
Printed in Singapore by Markono Print Media Pte Ltd.

Chapter 1

A wish fish sparkled in the Wishwater River.
Sakura reached out and grabbed it. She wondered
who would get their wish today.

Wish fish made wishes come true. Every person had a wish fish that was meant for them. As a Wish Fisher, Sakura could tell who each fish belonged to.

She would deliver the fish to its owner so they could make their wish.

People often wished for things like wonderful feasts or beautiful clothes.

Sakura held the fish. It tingled in her hands and she saw a familiar wrinkly face in her mind. This fish belonged to Mr Tanaka!

Sakura could already picture what Mr Tanaka would wish for.

Sakura was born a Wish Fisher, just like her mother and her grandmother. She enjoyed being a Wish Fisher but she also longed for adventure. Sakura hoped that one day she'd find her own fish so she could wish for something exciting, like a dragon to take her on an adventure.

But for now, she was happy catching wish fish for other people.

However, when Sakura went fishing
the next day, she didn't catch
a single wish fish.
Or the next day.
Or the next.

Sakura had a bad feeling
in her stomach. Where had
all the wish fish gone?

Chapter 2

A week later, there were still no fish. Sakura rowed up the river to look for them. Instead, she found a ship. Its golden sails were painted with the Emperor's crest.

A heavy net full of wish fish dragged behind the ship.

"Excuse me!" Sakura cried. "You can't steal other people's wish fish!"

A boy not much older than
Sakura appeared at the rails
and sneered down at her.

"You're wrong," he said proudly. "I'm the Emperor.
And as the Emperor, I can do what I like with the
wish fish." He held up a fish and it began to sparkle.
"No, don't!" cried Sakura.

But the Emperor ignored her. "I wish for a storm to chase
away this annoying girl."

Chapter 3

It started to pour with rain. Sakura's boat quickly filled with water and she knew it would soon sink. She dived into the Wishwater River, swam to the Emperor's ship and climbed aboard.

"Why are you stealing other people's wish fish?" she shouted.

"Because I'm bored!" sighed the Emperor. "I have
to go to dull dances and royal meetings. I want to do
something exciting!"

Sakura knew how he felt. After all, she'd often wanted to
do something exciting herself. But that didn't make it right.
"You have to let the wish fish go," she said.

"Maybe later," said the Emperor, grabbing another wish fish.
"But first, I wish to fly!"

Chapter 4

The fish sparkled. The wooden deck of the boat changed to golden scales! There was a huge roar. The Emperor's wish had turned the boat into a dragon!

Sakura held on tight as the dragon flew up into the air.
The net full of wish fish was caught on its tail. The Emperor
sat on the dragon's back and laughed.

"This is so much fun!"

It *was* fun. But Sakura didn't have time for fun – the wish fish were still in danger. She crawled towards the dragon's tail, reached out for the net and …

… the dragon flicked its tail. Sakura tumbled from its back and fell towards the river below.

Chapter 5

Sakura landed in the Wishwater River with a SPLASH!

As she plunged into the water, Sakura spotted something
shining in the seaweed.

A wish *fish!*

A wish could fix everything.

But who did it belong to? If she used
somebody else's wish, she would be as
bad as the Emperor.

Sakura grabbed the wish fish and closed her eyes. A face slowly formed in her mind ... her own face! Sakura was finally holding her very own wish fish.

If Sakura used her wish to fix things, she might never get another chance to wish for adventure. But she also knew there was only one right thing to do.

Sakura smiled at the fish. "I wish to undo
the Emperor's wishes," she cried.

The fish sparkled, and the dragon disappeared ...

... with a loud

POP!

"WOAH!"

The Emperor fell out of the sky and landed
next to Sakura with a plop. There were smaller
plops all around them as wish fish landed in the
water and swam away.

"What did you do?" the Emperor cried.

"I fixed things," Sakura said. "Now the wish fish will go back to their true owners."

"No!" The Emperor grabbed a wish fish and held it up high.
Sakura held her breath, afraid of what he'd wish for next.
"Don't do it!" she begged.

The Emperor sighed and let the fish go.
"You're right … I suppose. These wishes don't
belong to me." He hung his head. "But I get so
bored at the castle. I wish I didn't have to go back."

Sakura thought the Emperor sounded really sorry.
He'd done the wrong thing but a life of boredom
was no fun at all!

"You know what?" she said. "I think that is one wish
we can grant without a fish."

Chapter 6

Wish fish sparkled in the Wishwater River.
Sakura bobbed up to the surface and smiled.
Everything was back to normal ...

... well, almost everything.

The Emperor appeared near
her, a wish fish in his hand.
"Look Sakura, I've caught
another one for you!"
he laughed.

Sakura had invited the Emperor
to come and help her catch the
wish fish whenever he liked.

Sakura held the fish and closed her
eyes so she could picture its owner.
The fish sparkled, and ...

... "I don't believe it!" cried Sakura.
"This is your wish fish!"

The Emperor's eyes grew wide. He reached for the fish but then he shook his head. "I've had my wishes. Why don't you use it?"

Sakura smiled at her new friend and wondered what she should wish for.

Once, she had wanted adventure, but now she knew that being a Wish Fisher was adventure enough. Maybe one day she would need a wish, but right now, everything was perfect as it was.

"Let's save this wish for another day," she said.

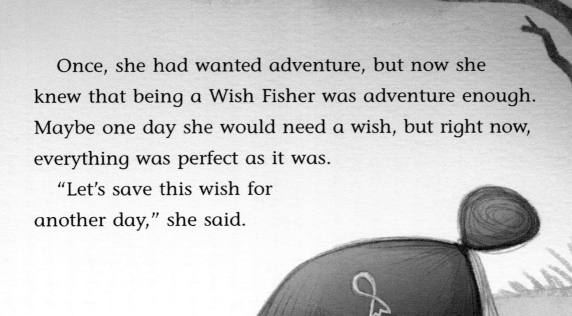

Sakura gently released the fish back into the river and together they watched as it swam off into the sunset.